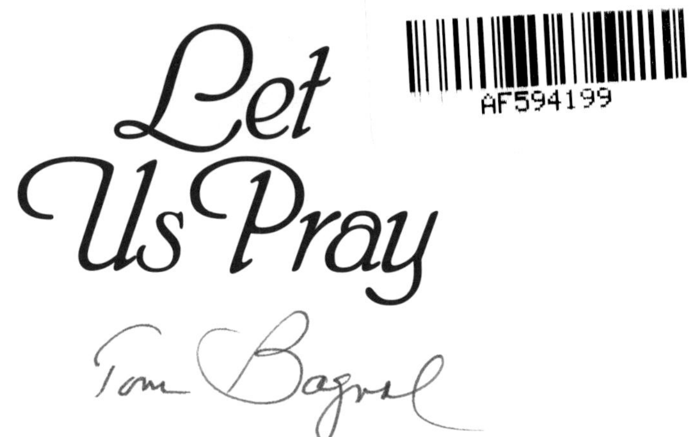

I Thessalonians 5:16-18
October 28, 1998

Let Us Pray

A Book of Uncommon Prayers

Tom Bagnal

PROVIDENCE HOUSE PUBLISHERS
Franklin, Tennessee

Printed in the United States of America

02 01 00 99 98 1 2 3 4 5

Library of Congress Catalog Card Number: 98-66926

ISBN: 1-57736-115-6

Cover design by Gary Bozeman

Cover illustration by Ben Bagnal

Published by
PROVIDENCE HOUSE PUBLISHERS
238 Seaboard Lane • Franklin, Tennessee 37067
800-321-5692

To

Catherine

my lifelong partner

who has typed every word I have ever written
and
to all for whom it has been my privilege to pray.

Contents

Preface and Acknowledgments ix
Introduction xi

Part One—Prayers for the Christian Life 1
Working Together for Good 2
Doubting Our Doubts 2
Having the Time of Our Lives 3
Your Attention, Please 4
The Wonder of It All 5
Pursuit of Excellence 6
Seek and We May Find 7
Near and Yet So Far 8
Foolish Is As Foolish Does 9
Put Us in the Winner's Circle 10
Life Is What We Make It 11
We Will Pray Anyway 12
Christians for All Seasons 12
Enough Is Enough 14
Faith for Moving Mountains 15

Part Two—Prayers for Greater Commitment 17
Promises, Promises 18
Till the Clouds Roll By 19
The Proof Is in the Prayer 19
On Learning How to Pray 20
Escape into Freedom 21
Be Still and Know 22
Keeping Our Wits about Us 23
Feigning No Fancy Footwork 24
Instruments of Peace 24
At Your Service 25

Lord for All Seasons 26
The Breaking of the Silence 27
Dreaming Possible Dreams 28
Praying It Like It Is 29

Part Three—Prayers of Thanksgiving 31
Human Divinity 32
Thankful in a Thankless World 33
Working Hard to Be Thankful 34
In All Things Give Thanks 35
Graceful and Grateful 35
Keeping a Grip on Life 37
Amazing Grace, How Strange the Sound 38
Thankful to Be Thankful 38
Not Forgetting All His Benefits 39

Part Four—Prayers for the Church 41
Honest to God Confession 42
For the Church Catholic 42
A Cloudy Day Faith 43
The Good Old Days of Now 45
A Silence That Speaks 45

Part Five—Prayers for Special Days 47
Freedom for the Captives (Easter) 48
Up to Calvary (Palm Sunday) 49
Bless This House (Mother's Day) 49
Grant Us Wisdom; Grant Us Courage (Independence Day) 50
The Advent of Thanksgiving (Thanksgiving) 51
A Time of Light and Music (Christmas) 52
When Word and Deed Became Flesh (Christmas) 53

Preface and Acknowledgments

PRAYER IS AN ESSENTIAL PART OF A CHRISTIAN'S LIFE AND WORSHIP. The phrase "Let Us Pray" invites the faithful the world over to prayer.

Prayer in services of worship takes many forms. In some communions it is formal, drawn from prayer books, the words old and comfortable.

In my tradition, the Presbyterian Church, prayer is more informal, often conforming to the style of the minister. Prayers are mostly spontaneous, unwritten, and unrehearsed.

The pastoral prayer, sometimes called the long prayer for obvious reasons, may have been given some thought and a brief outline prepared prior to worship. The belief is that there must be room in prayer for the momentary inspiration of God's Spirit.

I grew up under the influence of that model for praying. It never dawned on me that there was any other way of doing it. The same held true for preaching, always without manuscripts or notes. I entered the ministry imbued with those concepts and faithfully sought to practice them.

While a seminary student and during my first experience as a summer pastor, I was provided an opportunity to examine my beliefs and practices both in praying and preaching. It came as a result of tape recording my worship services that summer.

My prayers, I discovered upon listening to the tapes, were mostly meaningless jumbles of words that rambled around with no particular destination in view. Some of them were indeed long and usually covered the same subject each week.

I was doing what Jesus warned us not to do, that is the heaping up of words. I heard myself uttering sentences laced with every pious cliché in the book. While I believed God understood my fumbling efforts at offering Him the prayers of the people, I vowed to amend my ways.

Since that time, I have written all of my prayers in full and uttered them exactly as written. With practice, I have been able to develop a style that does not come across as reading or reciting.

My prayers are now much briefer, more focused, and better organized. I choose each word carefully using a more direct, less formal style closer to the way I normally speak and express myself.

While I consciously don't follow the traditional format for the pastoral prayer, that is—adoration, thanksgiving, confession, intercession—I do emphasize some of those elements in my prayers. For me, the single most important function of prayer is thanksgiving.

One unanticipated benefit I have received is the realization that the writing of prayers has become a form of personal praying. In attempting to pray for the needs, concerns, hopes, and aspirations of a congregation of Christians, I am actually voicing to God my own needs, concerns, hopes, and aspirations.

Over the years people have been kind enough to ask for copies of my prayers. Some have expressed a wish that I publish them. I do that now, with some trepidation, and with a deep sense of gratitude for the encouragement I have received.

Woven into each of these prayers are words and thoughts of those who have inspired me with their prayers. It is impossible to cite their names or to give them the credit they deserve. Lines from hymns, sentence fragments from books of prayers, and the public prayers I have heard are all a part of my own thoughts. I can only thank God for their inspiration.

I am deeply indebted to the Psalms. This greatest prayer book of all, continues to be a source of strength and help as I attempt to voice my prayers to God on behalf of those who accept my invitation to join me in prayer.

There are fifty prayers in this collection. I have left them almost entirely in the form they were originally spoken. It is my sincere desire that these prayers will prove helpful to those who, like me, have need of prayer.

I OWE MY DEEPEST DEBT OF GRATITUDE TO CATHERINE, MY SOUTH Carolina girl, who has supported everything I have ever pursued, encouraging me every step of the way in preparing this book of prayers.

My everlasting thanks to Carol Horton of Mount Airy, North Carolina, a talented and exceptional person who is literally an answer to prayer, for reading, editing, and commenting on my manuscript.

And to Peggy Wall of Executive Services of Mount Airy, North Carolina, for helping put this book into its final manuscript form.

I am grateful to my children for their encouragement and also to a host of friends who finally motivated me to take this leap of faith and put this collection of prayers together

Part One

Prayers for the Christian Life

"Thou dost show me the path
of life; in thy presence
there is fulness of joy,
in thy right hand
are pleasures for evermore."

Psalm 16:11 RSV

Working Together for Good

LORD, assist us in opening our lives to all of life, savoring all the moments, all the contacts, all the experiences that make up the daily business of living.

So much of life is ordinary and humdrum, so routine, that we tend to look upon it as having little value, something to put up with while we wait on the Big Event, the Special Happening.

Teach us to see life whole wherein all of our hours, days, and months are being woven like a piece of fabric, whose design takes form slowly, and whose beauty is revealed as the fibers blend their unique colors with each of the other fibers.

Help us to participate fully in living with no withholdings, no begrudgings, no hesitancy, and not merely as an onlooker. Let us make things happen rather than wonder what happened. Keep us alert, awake, and aware.

Show us the landscape of life as it really is with its valleys and mountains, its rough places as well as smooth, its broad highways as well as its straights and narrows.

Reveal to us that life always gives up its meaning as we live it day by day, not always in the great successes, the dreams realized, the major achievements, but in faithfully doing one's duty, loving one's neighbor, and by showing up to meet each new sunrise with anticipation and hope.

Lord, you have told us that all things work together for good for those who love you. Sometimes we are not sure what loving you means, or how we go about it.

Direct our efforts at loving you to loving our fellow human beings, which, we are learning, is the way we love you.

And teach us how to love ourselves, so that all together, life will indeed work out for good.

In Jesus' name. Amen.

Doubting Our Doubts

LORD, we believe—we think. Someone writes that the reality of doubt is not a reality at all, and is critical of those who tell us that doubt is a fact of life to be reckoned with. They tell us that the modern approval of doubt is not biblical. Well, it may not be biblical, but that doesn't change things. There are still many matters we are not completely sure of. Why this uncertainty?

We are convinced this vast and unbelievable creation is your creation. It didn't just happen. We didn't just happen. As surely as you made the universe, you made us. And while you were at it, you planted within us a loneliness for you. All this we believe. All this we know. So why, Lord, are there nagging doubts? Why these withholdings? Why this unwillingness to trust you all the way?

Part of it, we know, is our reluctance to let someone else, even you, tell us what to do. Like unruly children, we are aware that you know best and would always do what is best for us. But stubborn, unruly children that we are, we go on our way, rule our lives, make our mistakes. Now we are beginning to realize that you want it that way, partially at least, because you have made us free—free to choose which has to mean free to fight, and gripe, and rebel; free to get our kicks from bottles or pills; free to be slobs or tyrants.

You could have made us worthy, and it surely would have been easier. It's not that we mind doing right, it's just the daily frustration of having to decide what is right and being responsible for what we decide.

You could have made us puppets. But we don't want to be anyone's puppet. Not even yours. We want to be free, free to be ourselves, and we will just have to run the risk this freedom places on us. Now we see what it means to live in your presence, but without being manipulated by you, or having the right to manipulate you.

Thank you, Lord, for our freedom, because it creates the possibility of integrity, of genuine goodness, of truth, and love. Without the freedom to blunder and stumble, we don't have the power to become. So in your freedom show us how to become worthy, how to use our freedom to live as those you would have us be.

In Jesus' name. Amen.

Having the Time of Our Lives

LORD, according to the bulletin, this is the time we set aside for the pastoral prayer. We can use this time for many things. We can use it to see how many adjectives we can use to describe your greatness. We can use it to tell you things you already know, like how to run your universe, and how sinful we are. We can also use it to get things off our chests that are bothering us and for the confession that is good for our souls.

This morning we use it to thank you for some of the blessings of life that come to us in roundabout ways, blessings incognito and taken for granted:

That unwelcomed illness that made us lie down, as the
Psalmist said, and gave us time to reflect on our lives,
get our priorities in order;
That goal we set our hearts on that eluded us causing us
to change our direction and to find something better;
Those failures that bruised our egos yet left us
with a bit more humility;
Those times of frustration when we lost our patience,
but found it again, because we were forced to use it; and
those periods of heavy hanging doubt that led us through the
valley of the shadows and brought us out into the sunshine
of new faith.

Lord, we also want to use this time to pray for people for whom time is a problem:

The young, for whom time moves so slowly;
The middle-aged, who sense they are running out of time too
quickly; The elderly, who mourn the irreversibility of time;
For those only killing time, those biding time, those nervously
marking time, those in prison doing time, and those who
spend so much time resisting time.

You have set eternity in our hearts, yet we must live by clocks and calendars and schedules. Help us to recognize that we live every hour of our lives in your presence, making each minute a golden drop of eternity to enjoy now, a moment we need not seek to fill with meaning, because it is already full just waiting for our discovery. Thank you for this time of prayer.

In Jesus' name. Amen.

Your Attention, Please

LORD, there is a great sense of comfort in knowing how well you know us:

Our names and addresses, our zip codes, our social security
numbers, all of the demographic data pertaining to weight,
height, color of eyes, shoe sizes, educational backgrounds,
even the number of hairs on our heads.

This is a big universe, and it is so easy for us to feel alone and lost, and yet we are never lost from your concern and caring.

But there is also an element of fear in knowing that you know what unruly kingdoms lie behind our Sunday clothes and carefully cultivated manners:

> The anger ready to leap upon anyone or anything we let
> make us mad; The hostility reserved for those who fail us,
> or disappoint us, or who upset our apple carts;
> The scorn poised for venting on the weak, unmotivated "less
> thans" of our world;
> The anxiety about our feelings of guilt, inferiority, shame,
> and pride.

Maybe it's really not fear of your knowing but of our knowing, for the persons we least know are the ones walking around in our skins.

Give us the courage to be; the courage to be honest, not because it is the best policy, but because our integrity demands it; the courage to be fearless; to give up the belief that we will not be good without it; to give up the fear that we cannot really trust ourselves; the courage to be ourselves, to find ourselves, to like ourselves.

Lord, we pray poorly at best. We would like to be so eloquent, so persuasive, so persistent that you dare not hear and answer our prayers. Yet we are ignorant of the fact that our truest prayers, our sincerest petitions, are many times those we struggle to voice, desperate outcries of our need, fumbling, awkward, inept, non–prayers, passionate and real. It's your attention we want. Don't overlook us. Let us know we already have it.

In Jesus' name. Amen.

The Wonder of It All

LORD, sometimes this Christian business is not what we would like it to be, especially when we are confronted with the truth that we are not what we would like to be.

It causes us to wonder why we are prone to love only if someone agrees with us, accepts us, doesn't make mistakes, speaks our language, is patient with us, makes us look good, and overlooks our imperfections.

It causes us to wonder why we will forgive, but with conditions, help other people only if they appreciate it, forget our commitments while expecting others to keep theirs, and condemn the sin of our neighbors while excusing our own.

It causes us to wonder how we would survive if you loved us as we sometimes love others.

Teach us to love as Jesus loves, when someone doesn't agree with us, when someone talks behind our backs, spreads falsehoods about us, lies to us, takes advantage of us, embarrasses us, and steals our thunder.

Teach us to love as Jesus loves when we confront persons of different religious views, different accents, different skin colors, different political and social beliefs.

We remember those hard sayings of Jesus when he said go the second mile; turn the other cheek; love your enemy; if you have two coats and your neighbor has none, give one away.

We remember those impossible sayings of Jesus when he said if your eye causes you to sin, pluck it out; if your hand offends you, cut it off. Be perfect as your Father in heaven is perfect.

No, this Christian business is not easy. And we are far from perfect.

What we really need to believe, Lord, is that you know we are not pure, not even close to it, and that your love for us is totally unconditional. For our failures, there is grace. For our imperfections, there is hope. And for our incompleteness, there is the eternal opportunity of becoming the persons you would have us be.

In Jesus' name. Amen

Pursuit of Excellence

LORD, we have been taught from day one that we are sinners, and we are made to feel guilty because we aren't constantly reminding you of it.

We are urged to humble ourselves and in our mind's eye we see pictures of pitiful people, groveling in the dirt, prostrating themselves before you in what is supposed to be a pleasing spectacle. We are compared to worms and have no value whatsoever.

Somewhere along the way something has been missed. There is a more positive appraisal of us, one more in keeping with our dignity as human beings. It is the one the Psalmist, inspired by you, recorded in the Psalm we number the eighth:

When I look at the heavens, the work of your hands, . . .
what are human beings that you are mindful of them,
mortals that you care for them?
You have made us a little lower than God, and crowned us
with glory and honor. . . . O Lord, our Lord, how excellent
is your name in all the earth.

Forgive us for accepting a status less than the one you have given us.Of course we are sinners and don't always attain to the lofty status you desire for us. So we seek your forgiveness that lifts us to our feet, that we may stand tall and straight in your presence.

Save us from dwelling on our weaknesses.

Save us from false humility. Enable us to praise you for your faith in us, the confidence that is the source of our strength.

Empower us to live our lives as those who have nothing to hide and no need to hide; as those who are free of guilt, and no need to feel guilty; as those who have no fear, because there is nothing to fear.

O Lord, your name, your character, your being is excellent in all the earth. Let us honor your name by honoring all you hold dear. Keep us from profaning your name by profaning that which is sacred to you, or taking your name in vain by refusing the good name you have given us.

In Jesus' name. Amen.

Seek and We May Find

LORD, with the Psalmist of old and a chorus of other voices out of the Ancient Book, we pray, "Oh that we knew where we might find you."

We have sought you sometimes piously in church but have not always found you there. Our minds are crowded with many thoughts, worries, concerns, and plans. Are you there somewhere, Lord?

We have often sought you frantically, when in desperate moments and situations we felt like life was getting away from us, like a kite on a string we let slip from our fingers. We feel the urge to bargain and promise and vow.Where are you, Lord?

We have sought you sometimes when awakened from a sound sleep, lying quietly in our beds, the house hushed and dark, our minds suddenly filled with fear. We sense that you are near, there amid the shadows. Are you there, Lord?

There have been those fleeting moments when your presence surprised us. We knew it was you, and then you were gone. Will you come back? Oh that we knew where we might find you. You are nearer than breathing, we are told. Could it be that we are the ones playing hide and seek with you? Perhaps we need to learn that we cannot find you with our minds or in our minds, or thoughts or fantasies, but in our beings, our spirits, our souls, that when we let our minds wander from thoughts of you, you do not vanish as though a genie.

So it is not where are you but where are we? You are always here,present in all places, and in all situations. And we are with you consciously or unconsciously, in or out of our minds, our lives indwelled with your spirit, our spirits touched by your holy presence, for you have long been with us, always loving us,always amazing us with your grace.

In Jesus' name. Amen.

Near and Yet So Far

LORD, you are never far from us, yet often we are far from you. From our world and its pressure and heavy demands, its sound and fury, we turn to you for peace, purity and power. We pray for more sensitive consciences. Through the wear and tear of daily living, they have become calloused and hard; enliven them by your presence.

Hear us as we confess to you our careless regard for those who are part of our lives:

> If we have let someone down who trusted us, if we have
> brought pain and inconvenience to another person by
> our thoughtlessness;
> if we have hurt someone's feelings, we ask your forgiveness.
> If we have stepped on someone in order to be taller,
> or used someone for our own selfish purposes, convict us
> and motivate us to seek their forgiveness while we are
> seeking your forgiveness.

We pray for those who cannot or do not pray for themselves, those for whom prayer has no meaning, those for whom prayer is only words floating in empty space where there are no ears to hear. Forgive us if there are those who are unable to see your power at work in our lives, or so little of it, they assume no power is available.

We pray for peace in a world where the futility and insanity of violence and hatred are ways of life. "Cure your children's warring madness,"and "let our ordered lives confess the beauty of your peace." Now hear us, each of us, as we offer to you, in the silence of our hearts,our most intimate prayers, our private prayers, for our own needs, and the needs of those whom we love.

(Silence)

In Jesus' name. Amen.

Foolish Is As Foolish Does

LORD, because we did not create ourselves; because we are not totally self-sufficient, because we cannot forgive ourselves, we reach out to you, our creator, our helper, our redeemer.

We thank you for the world you have created and given us to use and enjoy, and to preserve for future generations. We confess our mismanagement of your world, our shortsighted use of its natural resources, the depletion of the ozone layer that protects us from harmful rays of the sun, the contamination of the air we breathe, the indiscriminate destruction of the green spaces that help balance the ecology, the pollution of our streams and rivers and great bodies of water.

Awaken in us a deep sense of our stewardship of the creation you pronounced good. Alarm us that we threaten to make it bad.

We need you every moment of our lives. Some of our weaknesses are so obvious as to go without praying. You know what they are before we admit them.Others are not so obvious to us, problems we must meet in ways that allow us to grow: temptations to resist, burdens to bear, patience to learn, doubts to endure, fears to overcome and faith to practice. We must know you are in it all with us.

We seek forgiveness and know we must be forgiving. How many times must we forgive those who trespass against us? Seven times? Seven times seventy? Help us to understand that forgiveness is not a matter of mathematics but of degree, not quantity, but quality. It must be complete, as you completely forgive us.

Lord, this is a most promising time to be alive despite the evidence to the contrary. We have the potential for an undreamed-of future where all God's children may enjoy healthy, meaningful lives.

Keep us from squandering our opportunities through ignorance, greed,pride, prejudice, and pettiness. Enlarge our faith in you, the God of creation, and our ability to trust you even when our nerve fails us, and we falter as your people.

In Jesus' name. Amen.

Put Us in the Winner's Circle

LORD, once again we come storming into your presence, trampling your courts, telling you how to run your universe, and we do so knowing that you won't throw us out or turn us away.

Throughout another week the world has towered over us with problems that seem only to grow larger. Frankly we are tired, perplexed, and anxious.

We don't like to think of ourselves as sheep, but we do admit we need shepherding beside still waters, green pastures, and all the rest. We need your help. So surprise us with some new thought, a fresh insight, and renewed perspective that will make this a better week.

Give us victory over our temptations. Forgive us that we seem not to be able to handle them except by giving in. Remind us how our lives are deeply woven into the lives of all whom we love, and what we do affects the whole fabric of our lives together.

Give us victory over our prosperity if it tends us toward selfishness and pride. May we be masters over it and not victims of it.

Give us victory in our daily work, that we don't become slaves to it. We thank you for work to do and for the possibility of finding meaning in it, as well as the wages it provides.

Give us victory over our leisure, that it becomes the pause that refreshes, that recreates, and revives us rather than dominating our thoughts and plans.

As we pray for ourselves, we also pray for all of those in our society who do things we cannot, or would not do:

> Those who work to save our environment from our selfish exploitation, those who protect our forests, tend our green

spaces, labor for clean water and unpolluted air, who pick up the debris of our throw-away-society.

Lord, make the Christian church more Christian. Give us a vision of our work so clear that we cannot help but respond to it. Challenge us with needs beyond the obvious needs of our own, outside these four walls, to the world around us, and beyond us.

In Jesus' name. Amen.

Life Is What We Make It

LORD, life requires us to live in the here and now and yet we have problems doing it. We know this is the only moment we have, this one, right now. We can't borrow time from tomorrow or cling to a piece of yesterday.

One reason we have difficulty with today is the belief that what we really want or need to make us happy or to fill our lives with meaning is just around the corner waiting on our discovery. Teach us how to be open to life rather than trying to shut it out, to savor every human contact, to experience our experiences rather than analyzing them, and critiquing them, and measuring them against someone else's experiences.

Keep us from erecting facades to keep life out as though we need to insulate ourselves from the very thing we want most.

Let us walk freely in the world relishing every moment, looking forward to each new hour, each new day with anticipation, knowing that even in unpleasantness, hard work, disappointment, pain and routine, there are the seeds of wisdom, and the potential for meaning.

We know life is never a bowl of cherries, neither is it all lemons.Life is what we make it, and we make it so much better with your help.

Help us to be aware of the joy of every moment, which is ours now and not just after the fact. Enable us to appreciate the past and not curse it, to anticipate the future and not fear it.

Keep us awake and alert; time passes so swiftly, sometimes we don't miss it until it is gone.

Lord, life is a song to sing; sometimes we get off key and hit sour notes. Sometimes we go flat. Teach us that our music need not be perfect, but that we can all sing for the sheer joy of singing.

In Jesus' name. Amen.

We Will Pray Anyway

LORD, it's a crazy world we live in, beyond hope we are told. So why pray for it? It's a world wobbling on its axis under the weight of billions of souls caught up in a maze of problems far too complex to grasp, much less correct. The mood of our world is going sour. The standard facial expression is a heavy frown. Worry, depression, anger, fear are inflating faster than prices. Cop-out and escape are attractive options.

So why pray? We will pray anyway. We are told we can't believe people anymore. They will lie to us. Help us to believe them anyway.

We are told we can't trust people anymore. They will stab us in the back. Help us to trust them anyway.

We are told we can't love people anymore. They won't love us in return. Help us to love them anyway.

"Trust nothing," the cynics say. We are bound to fail,because the odds are against us. Help us to try anyway.

Goodness is obsolete. The good lose, and the bad win. Help us to seek the good anyway.

Dishonesty is the best policy. Hogwash. Help us to affirm honesty anyway.

We are told there is no place for humor or laughter in a world like this. Help us to laugh and laugh and laugh anyway.

And worst of all, we are told you are against us, a killjoy, and are punishing us, that you are either dead or non-existent, that you are a crutch we can do without. A plague on such thinking. We are going to believe anyway.We are going to trust and take that leap of faith, run the risks, anyway.

For we know deep down, intuitively, without need for proof, that hope is not hopeless, that joy is the surest expression of our experience of your presence, so we are going to rejoice anyway.

In Jesus' name. Amen.

Christians for All Seasons

LORD, we are not very good at prayer. We find it easy to pray in church but sometimes difficult at other times. We may prefer for others to pray for us rather than praying ourselves.

We have been programmed over the years to believe that prayer must always take place in a special setting, at a time set aside.

Nothing wrong with that except that it may prevent us from praying anywhere and at anytime we feel the need.

We can pray standing over a sink full of dishes, or riding a lawnmower, or driving a car, or sitting at a desk, or rocking on the front porch.

We can pray on the way to answer the telephone or anytime the need strikes us.

Thank you for being so patient and understanding, for hearing our prayers, for keeping that link with us intact, so that we know we are never left alone.

Teach us that we learn to pray by praying, and it need not be prayers of soaring eloquence, or pious words or phrases; in fact some of our most real prayers may be those that come in the clutch, or hidden in the minor oaths that slip out in a moment of frustration, or fear, or anger.

We thank you for the encouragement of the experiences we have daily with you through our faith:

For victories over our sin no matter how modest;
For insights and inspiration from your word;
For strength when we nearly faltered;
For courage to stand firm when we would have
preferred to collapse;
And for hope when we were nearly hopeless.

Lord, we are serious about living our faith. Continue to reassure us that we are becoming more faithful by the presence of your spirit at work in us.

We ask your forgiveness, as individuals and as a people:

If we have been overly dependent upon our works
and good deeds;
If we have allowed ourselves to lose touch with you in a
changing world that never stands still.

Make us Christians for all seasons, remind us of the miracle of grace, and never turn loose of us, even if we turn loose of you.

In Jesus' name. Amen.

Enough Is Enough

LORD, we continue to find ways to thank you for blessings of value not always evident to us. So we thank you for things we don't need:

We don't need any more mountains,there are already enough
to climb;
We don't need any more starry nights, there are enough for
us to enjoy;
We don't need any more spring mornings
or crisp autumn evenings.
We have more now than we have time to appreciate;
We don't need any more good books or great music.
We have more in publication now than we can say grace over.
And we certainly don't need any more great causes.
There are more waiting to be tackled than we have interest in
or strength for.

What we could really use is more awareness of what we already have, more anticipation of what is to come, and more gratitude for all we have already experienced.

Keep us honest with ourselves. Deliver us of any need to build ourselves up by tearing someone else down;

From expecting perfection in others while accepting
mediocrity in ourselves;
From seeing the speck in our neighbor's eye while
overlooking the railroad tie in our own eye;
From judging the honesty of another person while
allowing ourselves some latitude
with things moral and ethical.

We pray for all of those who need something we have, that we can share:

A smile, a kind word, a pat on the back, a compliment,
a thank-you note, a gift, a few moments of our time,
a sympathetic ear, a shoulder to cry on.

We want a kinder, gentler world, Lord. That seems crazy in the hard, tough world of today. But it can begin as we practice kindness and gentleness.Make us lights that shine in darkness, leaven that penetrates our granite-like culture, and salt that perks up our drab, insipid society.

Draw us nearer to you and closer to each other by the kind ministerings of your Spirit in our midst.

In Jesus' name. Amen.

Faith for Moving Mountains

LORD, we attempt to reach you through our words knowing there are no words that can convey to you the things we feel. The relationship we want with you is not verbal, but personal, heart with heart, person with person. So forgive us when after we feel we have said all the right things, we turn our backs on our fellow human beings, who, with us, must complete our relationship with you.

So out of the faith that moves mountains, dare us to believe:

> that it could even move us;
> that it could move us to do good without first establishing
> all of the criteria we think necessary
> before good can be done;
> that it could move us to love without an investigation
> of the worthiness of the person and calculating the interest
> on our investment of love, compounded of course;
> that it could move us from just hoping and praying
> for a better world beyond this one to working
> for a better one here today;
> that it could move us to a greater inner personal freedom
> of feeling deeply and less fearful of our emotions.

We wish we could enjoy the simple, uncomplicated, uninhibited kind of faith, the kind that can sing, "Oh happy day, when Jesus washed my sins away." We need to believe that because it states life's most profound truth in its simplest form—that one day when Jesus died and rose again, He made it possible for us to be free of the guilt of sin, the sin that separates us from you, and each other.

Lord, you have made us free people, but sometimes we prefer the restrictions of our old bondage, because we fear freedom and can't conceive of what life would be like without it.

So make us free, by binding us securely with your love.

In Jesus' name we pray. Amen

Part Two

Prayers for Greater Commitment

"Commit thy way
unto the Lord;
trust also in him;
and he shall bring it
to pass."

Psalm 37:5 KJV

Promises, Promises

LORD, we never know what kind of mental preparations we should make for this weekly pastoral prayer. When someone tells us it is time to pray, we pray even if we don't feel in the mood. So we place before you our yearnings that we can't fully identify, much less describe; our fears too personal to voice; our hostilities of which we are ashamed; sins we hope never get exposed; guilt for what we have done wrong or left undone. We do so in the confidence that you won't scold us or reassure us that you have children much worse than we.

We would like to tell you that effective Monday morning at seven o'clock, we will start being so good you will hardly know us. But, then, that would only be a repetition of the same old vows we make over and over again. It's not that we are tired of making vows, it's just that we are tired of breaking them. So take us as we are, convinced of our forgiveness, and begin right now to work something good in us, so that healing may begin, and the shape of a redeemed life unveiled.

Before we go away from here, we want to thank you for things you have done for us that we are just beginning to recognize:

> For foolish prayers you didn't answer because they were not
> good for us;
> For patience that we thought we had lost and found just
> when we needed it;
> For inspiration received from places where we never thought
> to look;
> For the love and kindness of people whom we thought had
> no reason to give it;
> For unearned friendships, some old debts repaid,
> and for surviving situations in which we thought
> we were "goners."

Lord, let us see again the connection between our anxious minds and our lack of faith. Drive out our fear save that of losing you, and then show us we need fear that least of all.

In Jesus' name. Amen

Till the Clouds Roll By

LORD, we bow our heads and close our eyes in prayer. Give us attentive minds as they compete with all the thoughts that seek to crowd out our need to pray.

We have lived through another week and have sought the fulfillment of our dreams and ambitions in the world. Now we bring them to you to test them in the light of your truth.

Here we bring our lives to have them arraigned and tried, judged and cleansed. We come boldly, yet with humility, knowing that you are a God of love and mercy who desires only the best for us.

We bring our doubts to you and the guilt we sometimes feel, because we have been taught that it is a sin to doubt. Teach us that when clouds of doubt drift across our skies and darken our lives, the sun is still shining; with prayer and patience, our faith will be deepened as we learn more of your ways and the ways of life.

We bring to you our anxieties. They are too numerous to list but you already know them. While it is a natural part of life to be anxious at times, we pray that we become less anxious as our faith in you grows.

We bring to you our sins. Some of them we hate and some we love too much. Some we want to give up, and others we want to keep, and hide, even from you.

While our sins are private, they have the power to touch and invade the lives of those who share life with us. Give us a sense of "God pleasing despair," an honest diagnosis of our condition, and a sincere desire to repent. Increase our confidence in your grace, and direct our lives down the road of health and wholeness.

Fill us with a spirit of goodwill and generosity. As we face the uncertainties of the future, of violence and greed at home, and hatred and war abroad, teach us all to love the things that make for peace.

In Jesus' name. Amen.

The Proof Is in the Prayer

LORD, we turn to you in prayer once again. Prayer, we are learning, is many things. It is proof of our weakness. We pray because we are afraid, can't face life alone, and need your help. We break up our lives into so many pieces that "all the king's men and all the king's horses" can't put us back together again.

We see ourselves as smart, self-sufficient, able and capable of caring for our lives and the lives of those entrusted to us. But then we are not sure—so we pray.

Prayer is proof of our finiteness. We are aware that we are creatures of a day, that our lives flash across the sky, glow for a moment, and pass on into the innumerable census of those whose history is marked in what we leave behind. Teach us to number our days so that we gain a heart of wisdom.

Prayer is proof of our sinfulness, not that it is sinful to pray, but we do expose some of the same sinfulness in prayer that we do in life. We pray selfish prayers at times, ask for favors and benefits from you that we may not think others deserve.

So in our weakness, meet us with your strength. For our fear, grant us your courage, and make us all whole, and of good health, as we give over to you more and more of the brokenness of our lives.

Into the void our mortality creates, come to us with the assurance of your immortality. Let us feel now the stirrings of that life you are offering us that death cannot end, that is of your own eternity.

And for our sinfulness, give us an honest confession and a sincere desire for your forgiveness, already available, needing only our acceptance.

Prayer is our response to the deepest and best impulses within us, so we are bold to offer all of our prayers to you in the faith that you accept them all, and answer them, not always as we hope, but always according to your will for us.

In Jesus' name. Amen.

On Learning How to Pray

LORD, I wish I knew how to pray. I would make such eloquent prayers that you couldn't help but hear and grant them.

When I think about it, I'm not sure any of us really knows how to pray. So many times we feel our prayers rise no higher than the ceiling, or evaporate into mist, and are whisked away among the clouds.

Maybe it is because we try to impress you with our eloquence, seeking to flatter you with verbal flourishes about your goodness and loftiness as though you need flattering or could indeed be impressed.

Maybe it is because some of our prayers are selfish, self-serving, asking you for things we could grant ourselves with some thought and effort.

Maybe it is because we pray sometimes for things that would benefit us at someone else's expense; or we pray for things we really don't need.

Lord, teach us how to pray. Teach us to pray for our real needs and not just our desires. But then you will need to teach us how to know the difference between our needs and our desires.

Teach us that prayer is not begging for favors or pleading for help, or when we find ourselves in some foxhole of our own making, suddenly realizing our need for you.

Teach us that sometimes our best, most authentic prayers are those desperate cries for help uttered in a minor blasphemy, or through clenched teeth, when we finally realize our sinfulness and our inability to save ourselves.

Teach us that, in the final analysis, all our prayers are acceptable to you no matter what form they take, no matter how selfish, or jumbled or foolish, because you in your infinite knowledge know us inside and out, and know our real needs even before we ask.

Teach us that we must never stop praying, or trying to pray better, because you have told us to pray without ceasing.

Teach us how to pray with the assurance that your presence is our greatest need and comfort, that you love us better than we love ourselves, and that you never refuse to hear us, even our poorest, most selfish prayer.

In Jesus' name. Amen.

Escape into Freedom

LORD, you have searched us and known us, as the psalmist reminds us. You know when we sit down and when we rise up. You know our thoughts before we do. You know where we are going before we decide. You know what we are going to say before we say it. You are before us, and behind us. You are above us, and in us.

Such knowledge is too much for us. It is more than we can comprehend. It may be more than we feel we need or can handle. We might appreciate a little privacy.

So what do we do when we would like to escape from you and have some freedom?

If we climb the highest mountain, you are there. If we go deep into the earth, you will find us. If we buy a ticket and fly as far as an airplane can take us, you will be there waiting for us.

In the darkest place we can find, so dark we could even hide from ourselves, it is as light to you, and our foulest deeds, most secret sins, most closely guarded thoughts and fantasies, are to you an open book and flashing neon sign.

Such knowledge may be wonderful, but it is also disturbing and may be our greatest terror.

Help us realize how wrong we are about your knowledge of us and your concern and love for us, that what we fear most is our greatest hope; our deepest dread, the surest claim upon your grace. Such a paradox is beyond us. It contradicts all reason and throws us completely upon your mercy and calls us to our deepest faith and trust.

Here this morning, we are most vulnerable, most exposed and defenseless. Help us experience your holy Presence as healing and wholeness, to know the power of forgiveness, and the victory that comes by surrendering ourselves to you, just as we are, without fighting or fleeing.

In Jesus' name. Amen.

Be Still and Know

LORD, who makes us see when our eyes are closed, to hear when silence reigns, to feel when our senses are numb, and to taste when life becomes sour, we confess how often with our eyes wide open, we refuse to see, with our ears attuned we do not listen, with our feelings sensitive, we decline to reach out, and with our souls hungering and thirsting for you, we hesitate to taste and drink.

Give us a wider and more inclusive view of the world. Save us from the tunnel vision that sees little beyond ourselves. Keep us from filtering out the harsh sounds of life, but to hear them with compassion and understanding.

Enable us to touch that which we thought untouchable, to feel that which we feared might hurt too much, to share the pain of those whose lives are filled with it. Help us to respond to human frailty and failure as we do to human hope and aspiration.

Create in us a thirst for your righteousness and truth, especially for your word, which is sweeter than honey in our mouths, as the psalmist of old told us.

Lord, we know we cannot conform our lives to your will unless we are willing to change and amend our ways. May we confess our sin to you honestly and confidently, and feel the cleansing power of your forgiveness.

And now we would be still and silent, opening our lives to you, in your eternal Presence, hearing nothing, empty of all ideas and images, just being here as we are in the silence of faith.

(Silence)

In Jesus' name. Amen

Keeping Our Wits about Us

LORD, we praise you,not just with our lips, for we learned long ago how easy and ineffective that is, but with a life that is motivated by your Spirit at work within us.

We know that even as we seek to praise you, our lives reflect the struggles going on within us. So we confess to you now that we do not like it when we see no return on our investment of love in other people. Sometimes we are angry when people don't perform as we expect them to. Our blood pressure elevates when the people we are called upon to love show us their hatred in return.

It hurts us when our deeds of love go unnoticed, for we all want a little recognition. We are serious about our desire and commitment to love you and our neighbor, so we will keep on trying, succeeding at times and failing at others. It gives us confidence and encourages us not to give up, knowing that you never give up on us, and our moments of failure bring with them the offer of forgiveness and growth.

These days of national and international turmoil require more patience than we can muster. There are so many things going on in so many places and brought to us by instant communication that we despair of trying to cope and understand.

So while we struggle to keep our wits about us and do more than just pay lip service to our faith: Strengthen our faith in your control of history, so that we are able to chart with confidence your leadership in all events. And with our eyes fixed on eternal truths, we are still able to see the spires of that city that lies beyond the rim of the sky; the city which has foundations whose builder and maker is God.

We offer our prayer in faith and in the name of him whom we call Lord.

In Jesus' name. Amen.

Feigning No Fancy Footwork

LORD, who created a world on which winter and summer show their faces at the same time, when we come upon dark days, when the meaning of life seems hidden behind ominous clouds, let us remember that the sun is still shining somewhere, and let us know your grace so we may not lose the goodness of life when the elements of our experience seem contradictory.

Keep us in faith so we may not pin all our hopes on any one day in life, but expect from you the gift of courage in the face of trial, and the gift of peace when we have lost even the last battle to our enemies. But in the honesty of our confession that we need you and seek you, we must confess also how we don't need you and how sometimes we wish you would mind your own business.

We don't always seek you in determining how we will feel about and deal with our fellow human beings. We don't always seek your help in finding a realistic judgment of ourselves; we don't always seek you when we feel we already have all the truth and answers we need; we don't always seek you when self-preservation at all costs becomes the primary task of our lives.

It was you we sought when all the wheels ran off our wagons, wasn't it Lord? We sought you when the bottom fell out of our lives. We turned your way when we heard the sounds of a drowning person and looked around and found it was us. We hustled up that prayer when we felt the chest pain, or became concerned over a child, or heard the approach of some new problem.

Forgive us our "first-aid-kit faith" and stir us up to a serious constancy of faith in keeping with all the mercy and goodness we experience from you, even in the midst of our puny efforts to be totally self-sufficient.

We seek you now, feigning no goodness, trying no fancy footwork, but only stretching out our tired, weary arms and collapsing upon your breast.

In Jesus' name. Amen.

Instruments of Peace

LORD, in the world where we live, we often forget you. Things tangible, visible, sensual, so preoccupy us we forget that spiritual things are just as real. Here in this familiar place filled with special meaning and good memories, let small things seem small, and great things great.

Rearrange the perspective of our lives. Around our days erect such horizons that the noise and the strife and the evil of our time may be seen against the eternal, timeless, restless love that still resides at the heart of our world.

We don't come to urge on you our small, self-centered petitions, but rather to put ourselves at your disposal. You are great, and we are small. Take us into your keeping. Mold us to your will. Use us that some good may be done to us, and through us, to other people.

We believe your desire for us is to have peace, a kind of inward peace like that of the eye in the center of a hurricane, a calmness and serenity in the midst of a stormy world. Let great Christian convictions live in our hearts. Blow trumpets in our souls. Give us such spiritual reserves that the gates of hell shall not prevail against us.

Give us grace to face our sin. Keep us aware of how our lives interact with those around us, and how our sin touches their lives as well as our own.

Quicken our corporate consciences so that we may repent of all those things that do violence to our fellow human beings.

Lord, our faith commends itself best when it sings, when it reflects the fruits of the spirit: love, joy, and forgiveness, that make the melody of our lives.

Across the boundaries of race and nation, over the prejudices that divide us, let your peace reign. Make us instruments of your peace, do-gooders in the cause of justice and righteousness, ambassadors of Jesus Christ to a world struggling to survive its own worst intentions.

We offer our prayer in the faith that has sustained your church and remains the hope of our world.

In Jesus' name. Amen.

At Your Service

LORD, from whom to hide is death and to know is life, incline your ear to us and hear the prayers we offer in Jesus' name.

In your silent presence we bow. You know the yearnings of our souls, those deep desires we can never put into words, yet, which struggle noiselessly to their feet at your touch, and stand before you mute with hands outstretched, knowing not what to ask.

Lift us to our full status as sons and daughters of our heavenly Father. Teach us that child-like faith that trusts where knowledge fails and clings tighter to your hand when questions go unanswered. Deliver us from all little things that bedevil us, the habits that hinder our growth in grace.

Rid us of all resentment toward other people just because they are different. Make us willing to see both sides of an issue when we are convinced there is only one side—ours. Keep us from being down on things on which we are not up. Make us easier to live with when we don't get our way, and when we do.

We pray for release from the eroding effects of unforgiven sin. Purge our minds of all memories that haunt us and the sadness that clings to our spirits like a dead weight. Move us to carry some burden that rests heavily upon your great heart, so that as we bear the burdens of the weak, the unloved, the lost, we find our own burdens lifted.

May we fix in our minds and hold fast in our memories the picture of our Lord, who knew fatigue, pain, hunger, thirst, rejection, and loneliness; who identified with our flesh, and bore our sin in his own body.

Keep us faithful to our calling as servant people of a servant Lord. Forgive us for the opportunities that have slipped through our fingers, for kindnesses left undone, the feeble excuses hurled at your feet. Hear our prayers for forgiveness and redemption as we pray together in the shadow of the cross that has lengthened across our world.

In Jesus' name. Amen.

Lord for All Seasons

LORD, who changes summer's warm breezes into the crispness of autumn, who lays upon earth's breast the snows of winter, who makes streams flow in springtime, and who in summer calls forth to fruit the sleeping folds of nature, be the God of all the seasons of our lives.

Some of our days fly by with creative work and meaning; others linger with their tiring demands. Some days we cling to with joy, others we turn loose with relief. Some end too soon, others never seem to end.

Strengthen and encourage us to live all the days of our lives in the knowledge that each new day is a gift from you.

Save us from wasting today by longing for tomorrow, by lolling away our hours in meaningless daydreams and fantasies.

Save us from littering our days with the debris of yesterday. Enable us to save in memory all that was good and meaningful while profiting from the mistakes, the heartaches, and headaches of those times when the going got tough.

As we struggle against the ebb and flow of the sea of life, help us to remember that it is the sea that finally brings us to our safe harbor in your love and grace.

Give us enough faith to cease worrying over the mysteries of life, and to learn to enjoy all that is clear and plain and understandable. And when our faith fails, give us new faith that drives out all our uncertainty.

As we move through the ever-changing seasons of our lives; our springtime of newness and wonder, our summer of vigor and growth, our autumn of maturity and accomplishment, the winter of our contentment and memory, give us the wisdom that life surrenders its meaning as we live it, hour by hour, when we commit our lives hour by hour to you.

In Jesus' name. Amen.

The Breaking of the Silence

LORD, you have told us to pray without ceasing. Yet when we need to pray and want to pray most, we find ourselves groping for words, trying to recall prayers learned in youth, and searching our minds for words that will convey what we feel.

Our prayers exist within us like seeds in the earth waiting for some prompting of your spirit to cause them to emerge into the sunlight of your grace.

Strength to pray often eludes us, some shame holds back our confessions, some doubt restrains our petitions, some lack of gratitude blocks our thanksgiving. Tongue-tied, Lord, we often come before you. Teach us to pray.

Break the seal on our lips. Unlock the gates of our souls so that our most heart-felt prayers may pour forth; so that confession comes from the depths of our being, for we have undone many a good thing and left undone many a needed thing:

> So that praise comes from our mouths, for you are the giver
> and sustainer of our lives;

So that we may thank you for the life we share with others;
For the work we have to do; for the blessings
of the past made possible by the hard work and sacrifices
of our families, especially the influence, the care, the love
of our parents, and for a future filled with the potential
for adventurous living and service to you and your world.

Lord, teach us that prayer is not a skeleton key that opens the secret vaults of your bounty, but a means of opening our lives to your presence in power and strength, as our way of breaking the silence, that pleads before you to teach us to pray.

In Jesus' name. Amen.

Dreaming Possible Dreams

LORD, so often when we lift our eyes to you all we see is the crack in the ceiling, the cobwebs or the need for paint.

Sometimes our lives become so cluttered with our schedules, our jobs, our schools, our homes, our clubs, our hobbies that it is almost impossible to be reverent, to turn our thoughts to you in a meaningful way.

We would like to do glorious deeds for you, but most of the time we end up having to iron shirts, or mow lawns, or repair plumbing, or put in overtime on the job, or study for one more exam.

We would like to be esteemed as devout Christians like Mother Teresa and feel the holiness she must have felt, but we don't have her calling or the opportunity to help a leper in Calcutta. And, then, we are not sure how holiness would feel or if we would like it.

We would like to dream great dreams and see wonderful visions, and inspire people to greater heights of love and compassion and mercy. But most of the time we doze off during our prayers and have our dreams interrupted by the alarm clock.

What kind of Christian do you want us to be? Certainly not saints or martyrs.

We can be priests, come to think of it, in that we can pray for each other, offer some sacrifices of money or time or talent.

We can be ministers. We can help one another, share someone's burden, encourage a young person, comfort a sick friend or just pass on a compliment or a kind word.

We can be prophets. We can speak the truth, discourage gossip, take up for someone society likes to pick on, and stand up for what we believe.

We can be teachers by our examples, by actions that match our beliefs, by the way we respond to life.

Most of all, we want to be authentic Christians, doing our best at whatever we do, seeking to grow, relying on you for strength and encouragement, finding meaning and purpose in the midst of our daily routines.

Thank you, Lord, for not requiring of us that which we cannot do. Help us worship and serve you in the common walk of life.

In Jesus' name. Amen.

Praying It Like It Is

LORD, wonder what our prayers would sound like if we really prayed what we feel sometimes instead of shifting into some posture of piety when someone announces, "Let us pray."

In a fit of honesty we might say that we would like for your kingdom to come, but not right now; perhaps later when we have more time; that we want peace on earth and goodwill toward people, but are hoping you can find someone else to work at it because our calendars are full at the moment; that you will deliver us from temptation, not all at once, of course, after all life gets pretty dull; that you will make us pure, not 99 and 44/100 percent pure, but enough to be respectable.

We are terribly concerned about the poor, the sick, the elderly, the drugged, the ignorant, the handicapped. We would like to see the naked clothed, the hungry fed, and the homeless housed. Perhaps you can find someone to look after those matters at least until we can fall back and regroup, and have taken care of a few pressing personal matters. You know how it is.

Lord, we have about given up on the problems of international politics and conditions in our nation. Frankly, between the Middle East and Washington our patience is about gone and we are verging on despair. Our tempers are short and our anxieties are rising at a faster rate than inflation.

You in your mercy and love can help us. You know that our real prayers are hidden in our attempts at living as though you do not exist; in the messes we make, the brave fronts we put up, in our selfishness, our tough exteriors, our pride. Help us in spite of ourselves. Hear our desperate prayers within and above the clamoring of our self-sufficiency.

In Jesus' name. Amen.

Part Three

Prayers of Thanksgiving

"It is good to give thanks
to the Lord, to sing praises
to thy name, O Most High"

Psalm 92:1 RSV

Human Divinity

LORD, we are grateful. Help our ingratitude.

Some of the blessings of life come in such plainly marked packages we can't miss them:

More food than we need, we sometimes overeat.
Good health, most of the time;
Clear minds, though sometimes forgetful;
Nice homes, some nicer than others;
Old and new friends, a great blessing;
Close family ties, couldn't live without;
  and your love that never grows weary of our
  presuming upon it.

There are other blessings, for which we should thank you, that come to us masked or making their way into our lives by the back door:

Those setbacks that work out for good in the long run;
Those unwelcomed burdens that make us stronger
  for their bearing;
An illness that destroys our notions of indispensability;
A dandy mistake that shatters our need to be perfect;
Having to practice patience in order to learn it;
A confrontation with a radical point of view that causes us to
  evaluate our own view;
A fit of anger, a loss of temper, that make us realize
  how human we are;
And feelings of guilt and loneliness that seek to drive us out
  of the far country into our Father's house.
We are grateful.
Help our ingratitude.

There are things we need that would make our lives better:

The ability to smile, even on our worst days;
The determination to persevere when the prize we dream
  of eludes our grasp;
The courage to keep living when parted from a loved on
  or a friend;

The faith to believe in goodness when the world tells us
 it is a lie;
The humility to acknowledge guilt and the willingness
 to accept forgiveness.

Lord, we are not as good as we think we are, nor are we as bad as we sometimes feel. We are human, and not divine, and sometimes it becomes a weight we cannot bear alone. So we rest our case in your strength and your mercy.

In Jesus' name. Amen

Thankful in a Thankless World

LORD, you are far above us and yet deep within us. Your presence is our life and we die without it.

We thank you for the ability to be thankful in a thankless world.

We thank you for our heritage as Christians; the hymns that sing of our love and praise, the broken bread and the cup that remind us of our Lord, the sense of community we share together here and in the world around us, the memories and connections with all of your people past and present, and our sure hope we have for the future.

We pray today for those in our society who are near the breaking point:

Those who are expected to produce more than
 they can deliver;
Those struggling under the weight of heavy debt;
Those who are out of work and find no job opportunities;
Those who face some difficult decision that will affect them
 and their families;
Those for whom their every breath is a struggle
 against some disease;
Those for whom temptation and sin are ever present
 and won't go away.

Teach us how to live one day at a time, taking each opportunity as it comes, changing that which we can, accepting that which we cannot change, and letting go of the past.

Give us possible dreams that keep us stimulated and manageable goals that motivate us. Give us enough success to keep us trying, and the kind of perspective on our failures that keeps us from giving up.

Lord, we need you in our various ways. We need an experience of your grace that will keep our faith strong. May our worship together refresh us, and send us out to live as those who know how to sing, "Our faith looks up to thee."

In Jesus' name. Amen.

Working Hard to Be Thankful

LORD, it is right and proper for us to praise you and to give thanks for all that life has to offer. We do find it easier to thank you when things are going well, when life smiles on us, when our way is clear, when it rains on our gardens, our lawns, our crops, and not on our parades. You have told us to give thanks in all things. We wish we could do that.

It's hard to give thanks when our plans don't pan out, when life disappoints us, when we are denied something we want badly.

It's hard to give thanks for grumpy people, unpleasant tasks, rainy days and Mondays that get us down.

It's hard to give thanks for unanswered prayers, for doors that shut in our faces.

Enable us to see that most of our problems have actually turned out to be opportunities, that we have grown and matured even as we failed and struck out.

In your wisdom you have given us more of what we needed rather than what we wanted. Sometimes closed doors meant open windows and thwarted plans led to better and surer goals. Lord, give us the ability to be flexible, to try another way when one is blocked, to be willing to look back even if something is gaining on us, and most of all, to learn and profit from every experience of life as those who know and believe that all things do work together for good for those who believe and love you.

Make us bold enough to believe that you need us, that you depend upon us to do some part of your work, that our calling is not to some monumental, earth shaking mission, but to being true to those lesser tasks that help make human life more human, right where we are.

In Jesus' name. Amen.

In All Things Give Thanks

LORD, we thank you, for the praise that is therapy and the gratitude that is the medicine of the soul.

We praise you for the incredible miracle of life that continues to find meaning and purpose, beauty and joy, in a world that for all appearances is losing its mind.

We praise you for your stubborn love that never gives up on us, the love we often spurn, and for the persistent spirit that fills us with hope even when there seems to be no reason.

We thank you for surrounding us with friends, for trusting us with free wills, for consciences that goad us, for families that nurture us, and for the grace of your forgiveness that comes like a spring rain when our sins become more than we can bear. We thank you for that piece of eternity within us that reaches out to you, the Eternal One.

We thank you for the company of good books, the inspiration of music, the release of laughter, for the fun of a game, and the autumn weather that turns the leaves to flame.

We thank you for the pain that heals, the food that nourishes, the sleep that renews, the schedule that orders us, the routine that steadies us, the duty that dogs us, and the rules that guide us.

We thank you for the rain that makes our gardens grow, the beauty of the winter snow that hobbles our cities, the winter wind that chills our bones, and the wood that warms our hearthsides.

We thank you for the job that pays us, the house that shelters us, the telephone that connects us, and the automobile that transports us.

We thank you for all things new that change us, for old things that comfort us, for our family trees that identify us, and for the future that challenges us.

And we thank you for this moment, that will never come again, that has been ours to praise and thank you.

In Jesus' name. Amen.

Graceful and Grateful

LORD, we live under your rule and are upheld by your grace; let all that is within us bless your holy name. There is so much of life that we take for granted and yet depend wholly upon:

The firm ground beneath our feet;
The rising and setting of the sun;
The seasons that march in predictable succession;
The seed that springs to life and bears its fruit;
The certainty of family love;
The dependability of friendship;
The gates of mercy that are ever open to us in our need.

We thank you for all that is new and changing in our lives:

The breakthroughs in medical science that are keeping us well and extending our lives;
The work of biblical scholars and archaeologists that continue to shed light on the ancient record and provide new insights into the Bible;
The advances of modern psychology that help us understand what makes people tick.

We thank you also, for all that is old and unchanging in our lives:

For sunsets; for precious memories;
For music; for literature;
For the call of duty; the need for morals;
For schedules to keep and things to do, and things we don't have to do;
For your word that endures forever;
For your church against which the gates of hell shall not prevail.

Lord, we pray for ourselves. You know our names, our needs, and our natures. We confess with shame, but without fear, our pride, our selfishness, our love of ease, our petty jealousies.

We need your forgiving mercy everyday. When we lie down to sleep each night, we need the quiet assurance of your comforting, guarding presence. And should it turn out that we will not awaken to greet the new day, we know that our destiny is safe in your hands, that we will indeed arise clothed in the shining mercy of our God.

In Jesus' name. Amen.

Keeping a Grip on Life

LORD, you are the hope of all who seek you and the joy of those who are found by you. We are a diverse group gathered here this morning, in age and outlook, in likes and dislikes, in needs and desires. Grant to each what you determine we need most.

We thank you for our time in history. It is as good as any and better than most. We have enough problems to last us, but we are also blessed beyond the dreams of any previous generation.

Keep us from losing our grip on life because of all of the evil we see around us. Keep us from losing our balance because evil seems to prosper while goodness is being sorely tested.

Give us the vision to see through the way things seem to the way things really are. Enable us to keep the faith as others around us seem to be losing it. Renew in us an ability to trace your sovereign will and rule in history that cause even the evil of humankind to bless your name.

We thank you for all the evidences of goodness we experience every day and sometimes forget to acknowledge:

> For an old and good memory that surfaces in our minds
> refreshing us in a time of need;
> For the appearance of an old friend who reminds us of those
> good old days long past;
> For the voice of a friend or loved one taking the time to check
> on us and to assure us of their love and concern;
> For a note of encouragement when we were down that gave
> us a lift.

Keep us always mindful of those who are not as fortunate as we. When we are warm, may we remember those who are cold; when we are full, may we remember those who have little food; when we see a beautiful sight, may we remember the blind; when beautiful harmonies fill our ears and souls, keep us aware of those who do not hear. Stay close to us, encourage us, give our hope, patience and our faith, wings,

> until the fever of life is over, and our work on earth is done,
> and we rest forever in your everlasting arms.

In Jesus' name. Amen.

Amazing Grace, How Strange the Sound

LORD, look upon your people with mercy and patience as we pray, for we are a puzzle to ourselves, easily buffeted by harmful desires and prone to doubt. Let this act of prayer be a turning to you and a means of grace.

We thank you that we are made in your image, an image that may be badly distorted at times, but an image that assures us we belong to you.

We thank you that you have pledged your care of us, that no matter what our circumstances may be, you are our refuge and underneath are your everlasting arms.

We thank you that your grace is greater than our sin, and no matter how dark may be the night of our souls, or how keen may be the sense of our failures, or how sharp may be the pain of our defeats, your healing surrounds us, your word stands sure, and your peace is real.

We wait before you in need of stimulation, of motivation, of new power for the living of each day.

Where we have allowed our hope to expire, rouse us from our gloom with the notes of yet another reveille.

Where we live too close to the bad news of our day bombarding us by television, radio and newspapers, remind us forcefully once again, whose world it is and whose hand is on the tiller.

Where the illness or death of a loved one brings with it the closing of a comfortable and lovely chapter of life, guide us into the near and new future with the assurance of your presence.

And when we allow the sour notes and discords of life to confuse the great harmony of our lives, teach us how to sing your praises, on key, and in harmony with our fellow human beings.

Let the music of our lives be acceptable to you, O Lord, our strength and our redeemer.

Grant us, Lord, to see you more clearly and to love you more dearly, day by day.

In Jesus' name. Amen

Thankful to Be Thankful

LORD, we feel thankful this morning. Our paper came on time, our coffee was hot, the arthritis is better. We rested pretty well last night, and we managed to make it to church one more time.

We are also thankful for our breath and bread, for the ability to remember and also to forget, for the capacity to hope and cope, to plan, to dream, to change our minds. We thank you for the serious minds among us who grapple with tall questions, the comedians among us who make us laugh.

We are thankful for duty-bound folk who are always on time, who remember dates, names, appointments and for those compulsive souls who keep us on our toes.

We are thankful for friends who remember our birthdays, who return our books, who accept us, and trust us, and bring out the best in us. We are thankful for the capacity to be thankful in a world of greed, hatred and ingratitude.

We are concerned about inflation but we are also concerned about deflation and things that are in decline:

For the lowering of confidence in our leaders;
For the depleting natural resources of patience, morality, kindness and manners;
For waning interests in learning, in discipline;
For those whose self-confidence has been shaken by failure, whose self-esteem has been lessened by the prejudices of others;
For dreams dashed by skepticism and hopes lowered by doubt.

Lord, we are told that things which decline may be revived.

Our faith teaches us of an optimism born in your great heart, whose nature it is to be constantly making something out of nothing, who makes things go that won't go, who patches broken hearts, lifts up vanquished warriors, dries the tears of the bereaved.

In your goodness we are upheld. In our faith you are making us whole again.

In Jesus' name. Amen.

Not Forgetting All His Benefits

LORD, we find your name upon our lips, because you first put the longing for you in our hearts and minds. We cannot escape your great love for us and don't want to. We know our pasts are in your hands, and we have experienced your forgiveness. We know the present is ours to use and shape and enjoy because you want us to and are in it with us. And we know we have no future except as you give it to us and make it safe for us.

We thank you for minds that can remember and forget, that can plan and change plans, that can recall a lifetime of precious memories and allow us to relive them.

We thank you for hearts that feel, that know no limit to the number of people we can love, that can overrule our heads when we are in danger of being too logical, and too rational, and too cold.

We thank you for hands that caress and soothe, that hammer and saw, that cook and clean, that make music and hold the pen that writes poetry and books, that guide the scalpel, that earn a living. We thank you for feet that transport us to our places of work, that can dance and run and walk, and take us across the threshold of home when our day is done.

We thank you for purposes that call us to do good things, maybe even great things.

We thank you for associations and causes that unite us, that satisfy our need for fellowship and meaning.

And how can we fail to thank you for your grace that restores us, and amazes us, and causes us to become more of the human beings you would have us be?

In a day when our problems on the international, the national, the community, and the personal level seem more than we can comprehend, much less cope with, hold us securely in the palm of your hand.

Lord, you are always making all things new. So by your Spirit, renew our love and devotion to you and to each other, warm our hearts, calm our fears, strengthen our wills. Let Christ's love for us so rule our heads and hearts that our hands and feet are always at your disposal.

In Jesus' name. Amen

Part Four

Prayers for the Church

"I was glad when they said to me, 'Let us go to the house of the Lord!'"

Psalm 122:1 RSV

Honest to God Confession

LORD, we are so bold as to claim you as our God, our Creator, our Redeemer and our Friend. We have built a building and erected a sign proclaiming us a Christian church.

Yet, if we are honest, we can see the contradictory nature of our claims on you. We confess how we depend upon you for the ultimate matters of life while denying your concern about the mundane, seven-days-a-week concerns that make up our daily lives. While confessing our love for you, we often deny love to those around us. We love ourselves but aren't so sure of our love of our neighbors.

We have no monstrous sins to confess. We have neither killed anyone, robbed any banks, nor flagrantly violated the ten commandments. We have committed no physical violence.

However, we must confess that sometimes we fail to treat other people kindly. We make unguarded remarks about race or religion, jokes at others' expense, circulate unfounded rumors or gossip, and make judgments, forgetting our own vulnerability.

Since we can wound other people with all kinds of nonviolent hurts, make us more aware and more sensitive of the deaf ear we may turn, the unseeing eye we cast over the needs of others, the cold heart and sealed lips.

Enable us to be the kind of people who not only avoid creating disasters for others, but who live so winsomely that we might save others from creating disasters for themselves.

Lord, you have claimed us for yourself in Jesus Christ and erected a sign over us, the sign of the Cross. Keep us from pride in anything save you, from prejudice against anything except our own sin, and from loving anything too much except you.

Show us your will for our lives, your mission for our church, and when we grow weary, afraid, and lonely, your presence will be our strength.

In Jesus' name. Amen.

For the Church Catholic

LORD, we pray today for your universal church, shaken by the winds of change, faulted by its critics within and without, struggling with its mission, rife with differences of opinions, balancing budgets, and seeking to grow in its spiritual life.

Help your church to be patient with itself lest we plunge too recklessly into some new or novel mission. At the same time, give your church boldness and courage to stand firm against all efforts by those who would seize power for their own ends and those who would leave the field out of indifference and lack of vision.

Enable your great church to know what is negotiable and what is not. Keep us from losing our sense of your transcendence in worship by promoting some god of the commonplace; from turning worship into emotionalism and entertainment, and a concern for popularity and public relations.

Bless your church with sound scholarship; teach us to love you with all our minds.

Bless your church with compassion and concern for our fellow human beings; teach us to love you with all our hearts.

Bless your church with true spirituality; teach us to love you with all our souls.

Now we pray for all who are joined with us in the experience of worship in Christian churches everywhere. Unite us in a common love of you and your word, and a common allegiance to you and your world.

Make us honest enough to admit our sin, honest that we twist facts and truth sometimes; that we harbor grudges and ill feelings toward other people; honest that we envy the good fortune of others; honest that we admit our need of your grace but hide it behind a facade of self-sufficiency.

Now open our ears to hear the good news of the Gospel like those who are hearing it for the first time. Open our hands to receive your gifts of bread and wine; open our eyes to the beauty of your creation and the needs of your people; open our hearts to love you more.

In Jesus' name. Amen.

A Cloudy Day Faith

LORD, you are always good to us in ways both obvious and obscure, so we thank you for every manifestation of your goodness:

For your mercy that falls like rain on the just and the unjust;
For your word that speaks to us even when we
  aren't listening;
For your grace that we experience even when we
  are trying to earn it;

For happy coincidences that, in retrospect,
  are evidences of your leading;
For your hope that finds us even when
  we are hiding behind discouragement.

We pray today for a renewing and invigorating outpouring of your spirit into our lives, and through us, into your church that will:

Strengthen our belief in the power of love to conquer hate;
That will teach us, who can only cry, to sing again;
That will teach us, whose feet are stuck in the mud,
  to dance again;
That will move us, who have grown cynical,
  to feel deeply again;
That will motivate us, who have retired mentally,
  to think again;
That will stir us, who have become too serious,
  to laugh again.

Bless your church, Lord, with leaders who know where we should go and who know where they are going:

With shepherds who love the ninety-nine and the one lost
  sheep, all the same;
With teachers who live what they teach as well as they study
  what they teach;
With theologians who are dedicated to protecting the
  mystery as well as exposing the truth.

Give us the faith that enables us to see forever on a cloudy day as well as a clear one.

We pray for all believers who love you, and would love you more if we only knew how; teach us the infinite capacity of the heart to love infinitely.

We would love you more except for the doubts that assail us, when our skies are black with clouds; teach us that every cloud is indeed lined with promise.

We would love you more except for the overwhelming love of ourselves. Teach us how to find our lives by losing them for Jesus' sake.

In Jesus' name. Amen.

The Good Old Days of Now

LORD, we pray for your church, scattered far and wide, expressing its faith in a thousand denominations, a variety of church governments, a diversity of creedal statements, differing at many points, yet seeking to worship and serve the same Lord.

How easy we find it to fault the church, to criticize it, to bash it, and to run it down. We see it clinging to old ways in a new era, or else running to embrace the new in reckless disregard of the past; suffering from battle fatigue and often unable to get cracking on vital issues; at times embarrassed by its Galilean accent, and at other times totally assimilated into the culture with no salty taste at all; often given to deeds uninterpreted by words, or to words unaffirmed by action.

Bless, correct, strengthen, chasten, guide, redirect, so that in the thick of life, we may be your servant people at the points where your sons and daughters are hurting and need your healing touch.

Lord, today we are reminded of our youths, a strong past of friends and loved ones, gone from sight but fresh in memory. We are reminded of our homes, whose doors we sought when the last streaks of sun had disappeared in the western sky, where our young hearts were warmed with feelings of love.

We thank you for the quiet confidence of our faith in your steady purposes for us, and for a deepening appreciation of these good days as foretastes of an even more secure and blessed future in your presence.

Speak to us in this brief service, of things eternal, strong, unchanging, and true. Fill us with courage for the living of these days, and make us glad that we have been taught by Jesus to call you the same name he called you, Our Father, our Comforter and our God.

In Jesus' name. Amen.

A Silence That Speaks

LORD, we are here to worship you. You are the ground of all that is. You hold us in being, and without you we would not be. Before we were born, before time began, before the universe existed, you were.

When time is finished, when the universe is no more, you will still be. Nothing can take power from you. In your holy presence, we can only be silent, before the mystery of your being.

(Silence)

Yet, you have spoken to us. Out of your silence your loving word has addressed us, called our names, and given form and beauty to our world. Your word has given purpose and meaning to human life. Your word has declared us forgiven. Your word has freed us from the dread and power of death.

As we live our lives this week, we pray that you open our ears to hear what you continue to say to us; that you open our eyes to see the needs of people around us, so near, and yet so far; that you open our lips to praise you and thank you; that you open our hearts to love you and your world more; that you open our hands to do the work we need to do, and to work for the good of all humankind.

Lord, we admit we are sinners, not just because we sin, but because we live callously amid our blessings, and do not live up to our full potential as your children.

Inspire us to live our lives open to your Presence, to know the reality of forgiveness, and freedom from the guilt that can spoil our health of body, mind, and spirit.

Teach us how to believe, to trust what we believe, and to be obedient to our most trusted beliefs.

We offer this prayer in the faith that you hear us when we pray.

In Jesus' name. Amen.

PART FIVE

Prayers for Special Days

"I will bless the Lord at all times: his praise shall continually be in my mouth."

Psalm 34:1 KJV

Freedom for the Captives (Easter)

LORD, on this day of days, we praise your name. With all Christians past and present, we are rejoicing this morning that death is conquered, that love prevails, that hope reigns, that new life is present in the risen Christ.

Let no heaviness of heart, or dullness of mind, or physical ailment, or pre-occupation of self, or over familiarity with holy things, deprive us of the joy of the day.

We are mindful of those prisoners for whom the Easter dawn brings just another day to be endured:

The prisoner in a cell of iron bars;
The prisoner in a cell of chemical substances;
The prisoner in a cell of ignorance or prejudice;
The prisoner in a cell of fear and hatred;
The prisoner in a cell of debt and bankruptcy;
The prisoner in a cell of pride and arrogance;
The prisoner in a cell of legalism and self-righteousness.

Set us free of all shackles and bonds that bind us; set the prisoners free, and then bind us all securely to you with love that will never let us go.

Give us what we need to be your disciples.

Make us the kinds of Christians who attract others to our faith.

Form in us by your spirit, discipline, generosity, and compassion.

Make us brave Christians whose witness to the world reflects a faith that doesn't waver under stress or cave in to the pressures of doubt and unbelief.

Lord, we hover a bit cautiously about your promises, sometimes strolling around them, hands folded behind our backs, or stroking our chins, as we contemplate whether or not we could ever be so bold as to really reach out to you in a daring act of faith.

Deep down we want to believe.

Deep down there is apprehension born of uncertainty over how it might turn out.

Help us bridge the fear gap with the kind of leap of faith that gives in to our best impulses and leaves behind all nagging doubts.

Christ is risen! Sometimes we feel it is too good to be true. Today we would give up fear and doubt for the joy of faith and belief.

In Jesus' name. Amen.

Up to Calvary (Palm Sunday)

LORD, you are the source of all good things; you are our hope, our source of courage and strength. Give us the wit, the will, and the wisdom to praise and thank you for all of life. You are always calling to us out of a love that never ceases and a patience that knows no end.

Turn loose the hosannas that stick in our throats. Overrule the pride that makes us too rigid to enjoy a Palm Sunday parade. Bring to life in each of us the little child who hails our Savior as he goes past us on the way to his cross. Renew in us the wonder and amazement of the knowledge that he is risen.

Today we pray for all people who must live and work in fish bowls and under the unrelenting gaze of the press and TV news media.

We pray for those who seldom receive notice except when something goes wrong, for those who must live more exposed lives than we, who must perform tasks and achieve results the general public won't touch, whose life's work is a calling from you often without the benefits and pay of other jobs.

Grant light to paths of those who walk in darkness. Comfort those with troubled hearts. Reunite those who are alienated for any reason. Give us compassion for those who suffer and are haunted by fear, doubt, and depression. Most of all, make us all whole, uniting the conflicting forces at work within our bodies, our minds, and our souls.

Accompany us this week with your Holy Spirit as we walk mentally and spiritually with our Lord through his disappointing entry into the city, the cleansing of the temple, the meal in the upper room, the agony in the garden, the betrayal, the trial, the crucifixion.

Lead us in breathless anticipation into the garden where we wait to hail our risen, living Lord, once again, triumphant over death and all the forces of evil.

In Jesus' name. Amen.

Bless This House (Mother's Day)

LORD, we thank you for the homes we grew up in, the homes our children are establishing, and the homes in our houses now. Today we are recognizing that so much of your love for us comes to us through the relationships we enjoy in the home.

We thank you for our families, the influence, the nurturing, the teaching, and the correction we experienced and take so for granted.

We thank you for the people in our homes who were, and are, so important to us:

> Our fathers, brothers, sisters, grandparents, and the ones we are honoring today, our mothers.

We thank you for the permission we were given in our homes sometimes without even asking:

> To cry, to laugh, to tease, to yell, to pout, to argue, to make messes, to fail, to be lazy.

We thank you for the support we were given, most we presumed upon, enabling us to be ourselves, to make decisions, to be forgiven, to learn from our mistakes, for second and third chances, for not giving up on us when we ventured into some far country, if only for a little while.

We thank you for the people who cared when we didn't, who kept trying when we gave up, who had faith when we doubted, who persisted when we sat back, who worried about us, prayed for us, and sacrificed their time, their energy, and strength for us.

We thank you for the human love we experienced even as your love, and the human generosity as your grace, for all evidences of heaven within the four walls of our homes.

Your world, Lord, is a place where anything can happen. It's the world you loved and gave your son for. Through your love in human families, you are preparing us to love the world too, to enjoy it, to preserve it, to be in it, and of it, with the faith that overcomes it.

In Jesus' name. Amen.

Grant Us Wisdom; Grant Us Courage (Independence Day)

> Our fathers' God, to Thee, Author of liberty, of Thee we sing;
> Long may our land be bright, with freedom's holy light;
> Protect us by Thy might, Great God our King.

LORD, we praise you for all you have been to us past and present. You led our forebears on stormy seas to lands unknown. You have led us, as pilgrims and strangers in a foreign land, into each new day, unsure of what it will bring, but in faith that we are not alone, making each day an adventure of learning and maturity.

We pray for the courage of our convictions, the strength of our beliefs. In this world which seems at times to be unfair and cruel, that rewards evil and punishes good, make us wise as serpents and gentle as doves.

Give us the long view of history that recognizes your hand directing it, that opened up a new world when the old one was falling apart, that inspired people to brave the unknown in quest of freedom, who often gave their lives for a dream of a better place, knowing that those who came after them would reap the benefits of their sacrifices.

Today we pray for our nation, young in comparison to other nations, but old in its vision of humankind's eternal longing for a place where people are free from the bondage of tyrants; where we are free to express ourselves in worship, work, and a willingness to do whatever it takes to make our great democratic ideals a reality.

Help us keep this land safe for diversity, where all God's children can share the dream—the ideal—where our differences unite us rather than divide us.

We weep when we see how we have failed, how hatred and greed and bigotry continue to poison our national hopes and aspirations.

We pray desperately that all efforts at promoting goodwill, peace, and harmony among races and religions, politics and economics, may have success; that old-time patriotism will transcend partisanship and the pride of particularity. Rest your blessings on this nation as we grow weary of violence and long to practice the arts of peace and freedom for all.

In Jesus' name. Amen.

The Advent of Thanksgiving (Thanksgiving)

LORD, we are thankful in this season set aside to cause us to remember to be thankful.

We thank you for good food and drink.
  Let us remember those who are hungry.
We thank you for friends.
  Let us remember the lonely and the friendless.

We thank you for freedom.
  Let us remember those who are enslaved in any way.
May our remembering stir us to service.
May your priceless gifts to us stir us to sharing.
  Help us put the thanks back in our giving.

We pray today for those in our community and area who are up against hard numbers; who have little reason to be grateful:

Those in prison serving a fixed sentence;
Those in hospitals whose time left to live is numbered
  in days or weeks;
Those on hard times who must pay the rent,
  make a mortgage or loan payment by a specified date;
Those who have been evicted from land or a house and have
  to be out by a near date;
And those who must make a critical decision by
  an approaching deadline.

Lord, make us sensitive to those about us who face pressures that seem greater than their strength, who carry burdens much too heavy, those who need your grace to keep body and soul together.

As we move from the season of giving thanks to Advent, when the whole world lives with a sense of expectancy that something good and great is about to occur, save us from making it a season of stress, of frayed nerves, of too-full-schedules, of tired feet, and a mailbox full of bills.

Instead, awaken in us a childlike appreciation of all this season means, that which comes to us through the music, the tree, the Babe; even let the hectic pace remind us that the time he came was the busiest time of the year in Judea.

Prepare us to receive with wonder and amazement, the gift of yourself that came wrapped in swaddling clothes, lying in a manger.

In Jesus' name. Amen.

A Time of Light and Music (Christmas)

LORD, who came to us in glory through the humble birth of a Child in a stable, we thank you that the most common things of this world are revealed to us in the uncommon worth of your grace. We thank you for His light that still shines through the cracks and crevices of time, illuminating history with meaning and purpose; for the music that filters through our calloused souls and stirs anew, hope, peace, and goodwill; for the wise people over the ages who unite faith and wisdom in seeking a better world; and for the Child whose coming not only changed history, but our lives as well.

Today is a good time for us to reaffirm our need to hear the Good News again; of the love embodied in Jesus so that we need not just speculate about the meaning of love, but experience it; for our continuing hope and faith and assurance in the ultimate triumph of good over evil; and for the gifts of forgiveness, release from guilt, newness of life, and relief from the fear of death.

With Christmas almost upon us, we confess that we have given too much thought to gifts and not enough to the Gift, maybe even too much thought to getting than giving.

Save us from all Scrooges and Grinches among us who would humbug our Christmas spirit or try to steal it from us.

In this world where life grinds relentlessly on, shed anew the light of the guiding star.

Send wise persons among us to lead us out of the darkness of our days into the celebration of all of those who know how to say, "Emmanuel."

In Jesus' name. Amen.

When Word and Deed Became Flesh (Christmas)

LORD, Christmas reminds us of that time when your word became flesh. It is also a good time to be grateful for those folk among us who by their deeds make their words flesh, who make visible and credible the creed they profess:

All those who work earnestly for peace;
All those who are willing to live a scaled-down lifestyle
so they can be generous with those in need;
All those who stand up for and plead the cause of the orphan,
the widow, the prisoner, the oppressed;
All those who will not compromise their ethics
for personal gain;
All those who find a way to volunteer some of their valuable
time on behalf of their fellow human beings;
All those who are willing to share their own experiences
and knowledge of your Gospel with others.

We are especially grateful for those whose profession of your gospel causes them hardships, pain, and scorn.

We are still trying to comprehend your ways, especially the way you choose the weak things of the earth to confound the mighty:

A teen-aged Jewish girl to be the bearer of the Lord of Life;
A backwoods carpenter to act as Father to the Rock of Ages;
A band of shepherds to be the first to hear the angelic hosts;
And a manger in a dirty stable to cradle the Prince of Peace.

In this season of light and love, let the magic of Christmas seep through our life-hardened exteriors and slowly fill our beings with warmth and love.

We also pray for those people in our world for whom Christmas is the worst time of year:

Those who will miss it in a stupor of alcohol and drugs;
Those who have no money to buy gifts and no one
  to give them gifts;
Those for whom Christmas brings back a nightmare
  of memories of loneliness, of desertion;
Those who will be pushed over the edge
  into deep depression.

Forbid it, Lord, and forgive us that this wonderful celebration of life becomes the dark night of the soul for so many people in our world.

Use us as bearers of the Good News of great joy to those who desperately need to hear it.

In Jesus' name. Amen.